Barkley, Barkley, Where are You?

Then, **GOD** Reminded ME . . .

DEBBIE SOUTHARD FINCH

Illustrations by Kimberly Merritt

Ken, thank you for allowing me to be me for thirty-two years. Thank you for supporting me and doing what God has laid on my heart. I love all the gifts you have given me. My favorite gift is Barkley! I love you, Ken! Also, I love you, Barkley!

Mama and Daddy, I am so blessed God handpicked you guys to be my parents. No words can describe the love I have for both of you. You are two of my biggest fans! I love you, Mama and Daddy!

Jacob and Sana, I am grateful and thankful God gave you to me. I absolutely love doing life with you guys. Oh, the memories we have made together! I love you, Jacob and Sana!

Kambree, my Cupcake, and James, my Buddy, I love being your Lolli! I love you to the moon and back!

Belinda (like a big sis), words cannot describe how you cheered me on when I was doing God's will. You inspired me so much, and I cherish our memories together. I love you, Belinda!

Debra, you always cheer me on, whatever I am doing! You are the Ethel to my Lucy. Thank you for the great times! I love you, Debra!

I thank God for inspiring me to write this book. I pray it will touch and change many lives for Jesus! ❤️

It was Christmastime, and Ken and I were busy decorating and shopping for gifts for family and friends.

One evening we were relaxing in the living room. We were enjoying our beautiful Christmas tree and decorations and all the memories we had made together. Ken looked at me and said, "Would you like to get your Christmas present early?"

I said, *"Of course, I would!"*

A week later Ken and our granddaughter, Kambree, came home with a goldendoodle puppy! We named him Barkley!

Looking at the paperwork, we realized Barkley has the same birthday as Ken and I. Yes, all three of us share the same birthday!

As time passed, Barkley was potty trained and learned to fetch,
give kisses, and shake paws. He loves me with all of his heart.

Our grandchildren and
other family members and
friends love Barkley and he
loves everyone!

While getting ready one morning I didn't hear or see Barkley. He was always with me. I said,

"Barkley, Barkley, where are you?"

He quickly moved from behind me.

"Barkley! You were here the whole time!" I exclaimed.

Instantly God reminded me, Sometimes in those quiet moments you wonder, "Where are you, God?" Quickly I remembered,

"Be strong and courageous, and I will be with you wherever you go" (from Joshua 1:9).

Yes, Barkley sleeps with us! Ken always wakes up earlier than me. Each morning he shuts our bedroom door while I continue to sleep. He takes Barkley outside for his morning potty. Then Barkley decides to come wait for me outside our bedroom door.

One morning I woke up to a loud noise hitting the door. I got to the door and carefully opened it. To my surprise, Barkley was lying right outside. He continued to hit his tail against the door.

When I realized Barkley was ready for me to get up, talk to him, feed him, and play with him, I recalled sharing this scripture with Kambree and our grandson, James:

"Behold, I stand at the door and knock. If anyone hears my voice and opens the door, I will come in to him and dine with him, and he with Me" (Revelation 3:20).

I explained to Kambree and James that when your parents ask you several times to clean your room, come to the table to eat, or get ready for bed, they have waited for you. When you don't obey, they keep waiting until you do. God waits time after time for us to come to him. God loves you and me. He wants to live in our hearts! Oh, how he wants to be invited into our hearts and live there forever!

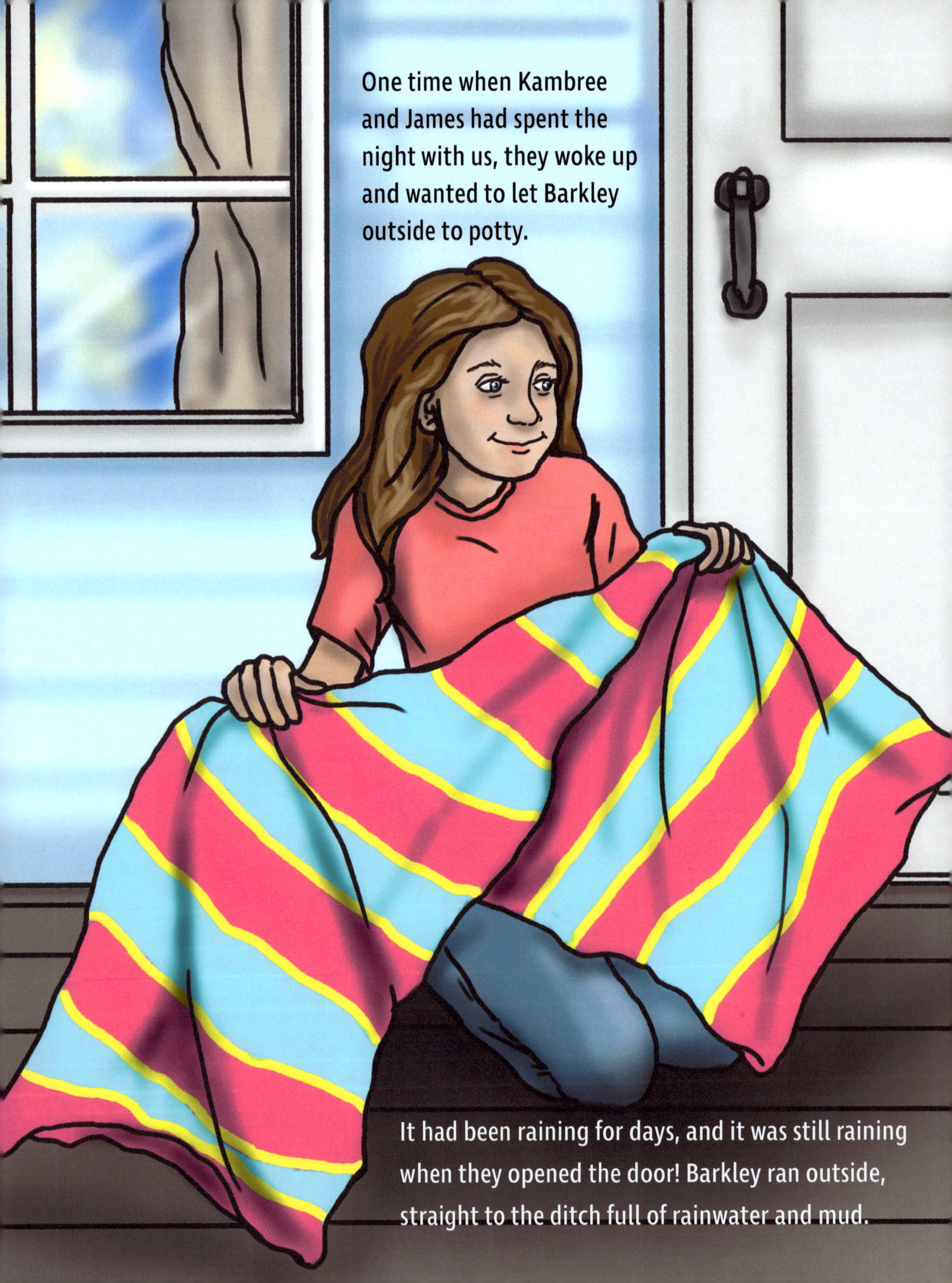

One time when Kambree
and James had spent the
night with us, they woke up
and wanted to let Barkley
outside to potty.

It had been raining for days, and it was still raining
when they opened the door! Barkley ran outside,
straight to the ditch full of rainwater and mud.

Kambree and James finally got Barkley to stop playing in the mud and come inside. Now he looked like a chocolate dog!

James yelled,

"OH, NO!"

Kambree hollered to me,

"GRAB THE BEACH TOWEL, LOLLI!"

I said, "It's going to take more than a beach towel!

He needs a bath!"

Ken, Kambree, James, and I took Barkley to a local store that had a dog wash. The kids wanted to bathe Barkley themselves. While they were bathing Barkley, I shared, "He reminds me of how we are filthy and dirty as sinners. God washes us and cleans us when we ask for forgiveness of our sins. He makes our hearts white as snow!"

Ken chimed in,

"'If we confess our sins, he is faithful and just to forgive us our sins and to cleanse us from all unrighteousness'" (1 John 1:9).

Kambree said, "I made that decision a couple years ago. It's the biggest and best decision of my life!"

I said, "We are so proud of you, Kambree!"

In a quiet little voice, James said, "I am proud too!"

BONES

A few nights later Barkley startled me awake! He jumped onto the bed and lay beside me. I tried to go back to sleep, but Barkley wasn't having it! He was panting gently in my ear. Surely I was awake now!

As Barkley breathed on me, I recalled scripture from a Bible drill:

"So Jesus said to them again, 'Peace to you! As the Father has sent Me, I also send you.' And when He had said this, He breathed on them, and said to them, 'Receive the Holy Spirit'" (John 20:21-22).

I realized God was using Barkley to remind me that Jesus gives me peace and the Holy Spirit!

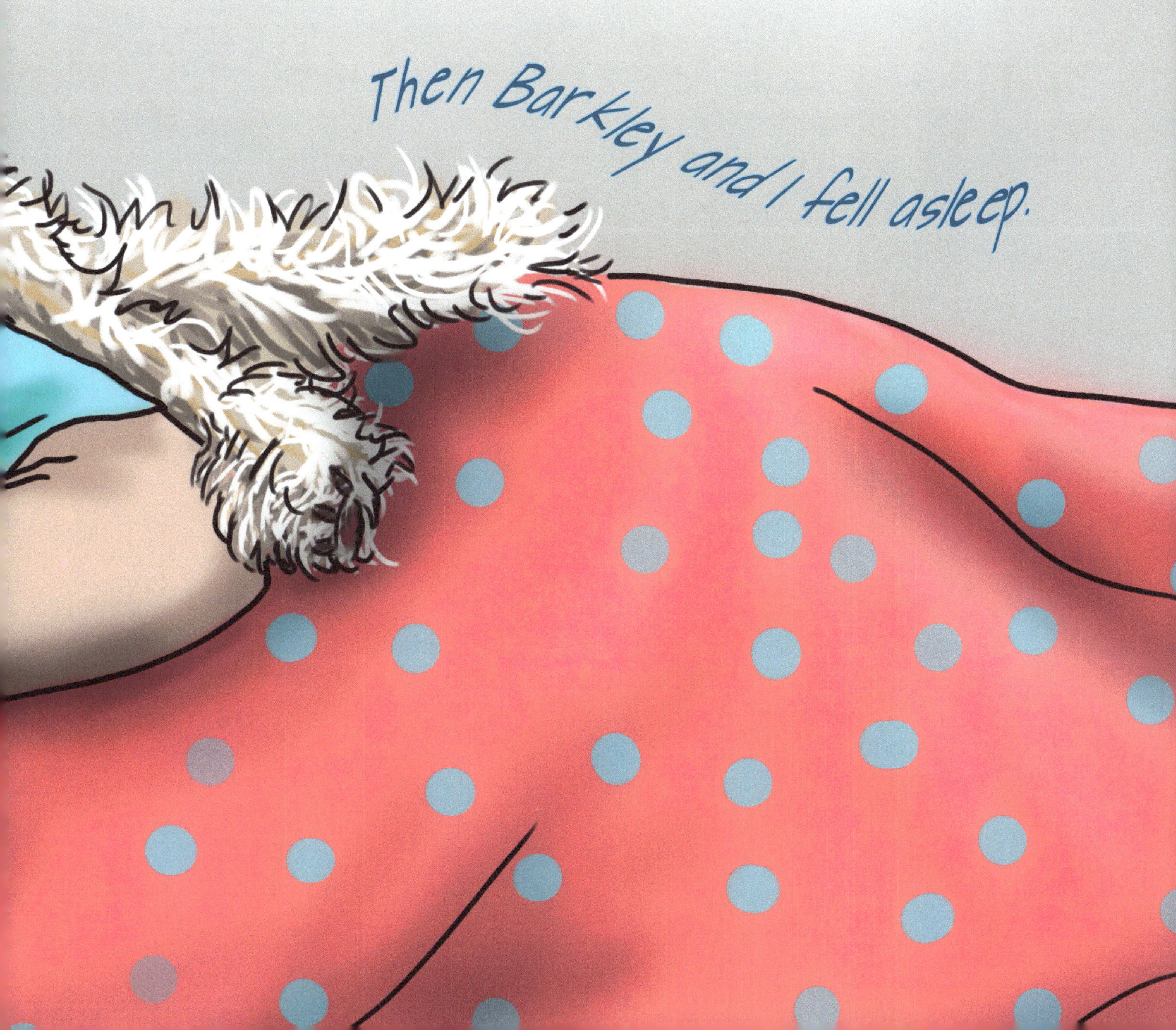

Later that day Barkley and I were playing on the living room floor.

Barkley stopped, **HIS EARS PERKED UP, AND HE BEGAN BARKING**

and looking toward the door. He always does this when someone is there.

Barkley protects me! He watches and listens to make sure everything is okay. It reminds me of this scripture:

"But the Lord is faithful, and
he will strengthen you and
protect you from the evil one"
(2 Thessalonians 3:3 NIV).

One of Barkley's favorite things to do is

jump onto the couch and lean over and watch the

beautiful fish in our aquarium.

He stays there for a long time. James loves to join him.

Once while he watched the fish with Barkley, James told me, "Me and Daddy and Mommy and Kambree went fishing yesterday. Daddy told us about Jesus wanting us to be 'fishers of men.' That means tell everybody that Jesus loves them. I know, because the Bible tells me so! We sing that at church and Mommy sings it to me at home. That's why I am following him!"

Barkley knows how to shake paws, but usually he lifts his paw and then sets it down. One day, though, he kept his paw in my hand and kept looking me in the eye, as if there were something he really wanted me to know.

At that moment God reminded me that no matter what is going on,

he has the whole world in his hands.

Just like my family takes care of Barkley and loves him unconditionally, God takes care of us and loves us no matter what!

Meet Barkley

Barkley, Kambree, James, Jacob, Sana

& his *Family*

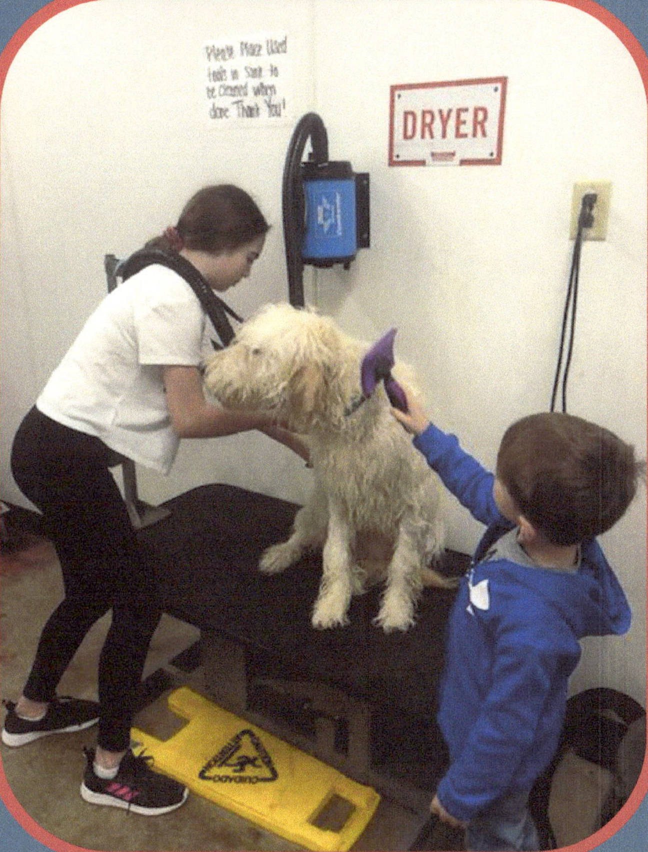

Barkley, Ken, Debbie